NATIONAL GEOGRAPHIC

T0061008

PEOPLE BUILD DAMS

Trent Johnson

PEOPLE BUILD DAMS.

SO DO BEAVERS.

PEOPLE BUILD TOWERS.

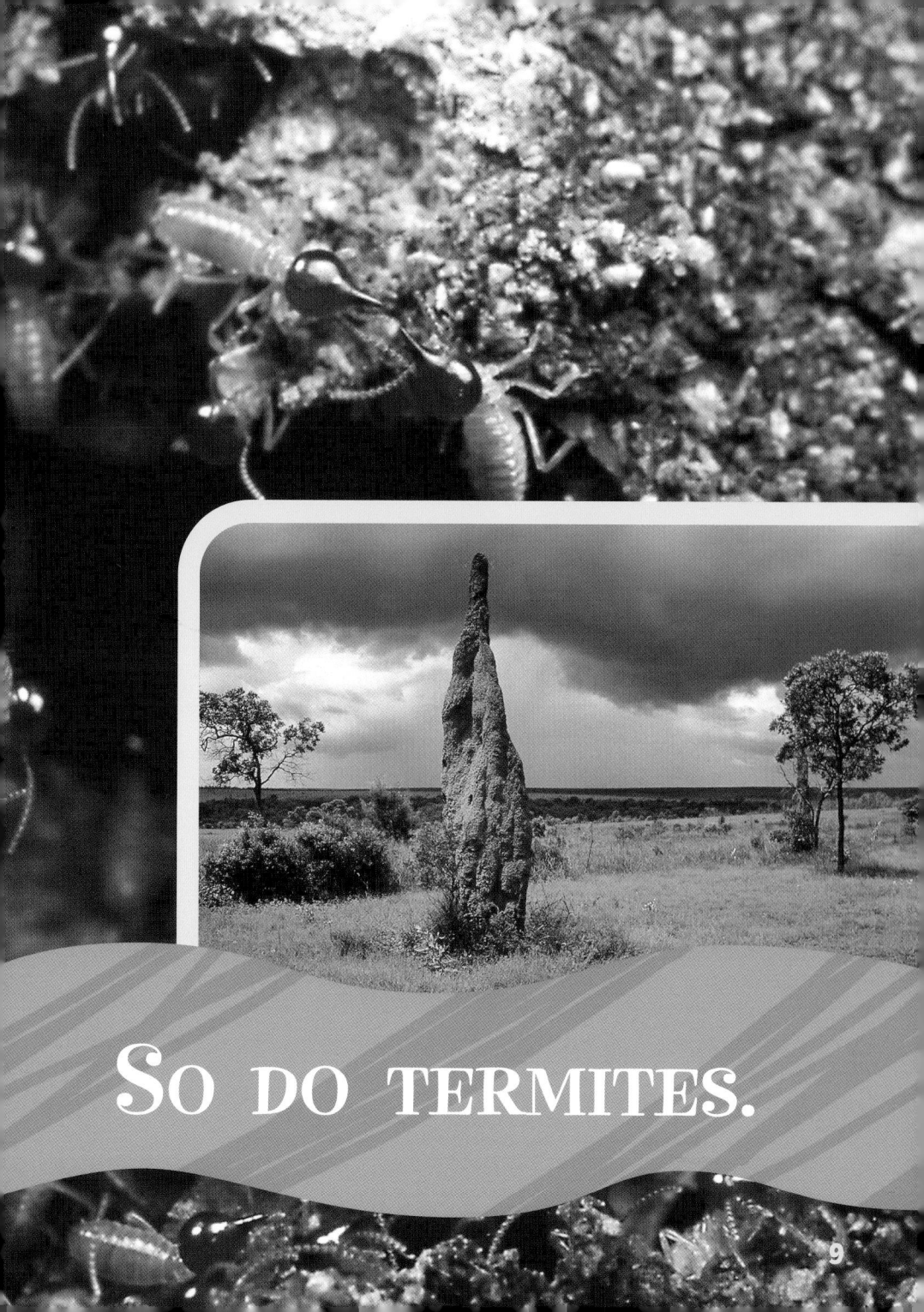

SO DO TERMITES.

PEOPLE BUILD TUNNELS.

So do moles.

People build places to store food.

COOKBOOK
Colomba
Milano
ANNALISA
Cous Cous

SO DO SPIDERS.

PEOPLE BUILD HOUSES

WITH MANY ROOMS.

SO DO ANTS.

PEOPLE BUILD PLACES TO KEEP BABIES SAFE.

twinkle
twinkle
Little

So do eagles.